MARGRET & H.A. REY'S
Curious George
in the Snow

Illustrated in the style of H. A. Rey by Vipah Interactive

Houghton Mifflin Company   Boston 1998

Based on the character of Curious George®, created by Margret and H. A. Rey.
Illustrated by Vipah Interactive, Wellesley, Massachusetts: C. Becker, D. Fakkel, M. Jensen,
S. SanGiacomo, C. Yu.

The text of this book is set in 17-pt. Adobe Garamond.
The illustrations are watercolor and charcoal pencil, reproduced in full color.

Library of Congress Cataloging-in-Publication Data

Curious George in the snow / based on the original character by Margret and H. A. Rey.
p. cm.
Summary: A curious monkey causes quite a commotion on the ski slopes.
RNF ISBN 0-395-91902-9   PAP ISBN 0-395-91907-X   PABRD ISBN 0-395-92336-0
[1. Monkeys—Fiction. 2. Winter sports—Fiction.]   I. Rey, Margret, 1906–1996.
II. Rey, H. A. (Hans Augusto), 1898–1977.
PZ7.C921675 1998
[E]—dc21   98-14162
                                               CIP AC

Manufactured in the United States of America
WOZ 10 9 8 7 6 5 4 3 2 1

This is George.

George was a good little monkey and always very curious.

One cold day George went to a winter sports competition with his friend, the man with the yellow hat. They were outside all morning and wanted to warm up with a hot drink.

At the ski lodge on top of the mountain, the man said, "George, why don't you wait at this table while I get some hot chocolate? I'll be right back, so don't get into any trouble."

George liked being on top of the mountain; there was so much to see! Why, there was something interesting.

George thought it looked like a spaceship.

He was curious. What was a spaceship doing on a mountain?

George forgot all about waiting for the hot chocolate...

and climbed in. A man in a racing suit saw him and said, "What are you doing in my sled?" He tried to stop George, but it was too late. The sled shot down the mountain—with George inside!

This is no spaceship, thought George. This is a rocket!

"Stop that monkey!" the man yelled.

But George could not stop. And there was no one to stop him as he sped faster and faster through the snow.

Suddenly the sled slipped sideways — George didn't know how to steer.

The sled swished through some trees

and whacked into a pole!

Luckily, George was not hurt, but this was not where he was supposed to be. Now how would he get up the mountain? George looked at the sled. It was stuck by the pole. He looked up the pole.

Now he could see how a little monkey could get to the top of a mountain. George climbed the pole, and

when an empty seat came close enough, he jumped!

What a view! From up in the air, George could see everything. As he rode up the mountain, he watched tiny skiers race down.

When he reached the top, George was happy to see the ski lodge.

This was where he was supposed to be!

George found the table. But he couldn't find the man with
the yellow hat.

Where could he be?

George looked down the mountain.

There was someone who looked like his friend! Maybe his friend was going down to get George. But how could George get down the mountain this time?

If only he had another sled...

Why, here was a monkey-sized sled.

George took the sled down

and gave himself a push. The sled was quick to pick up speed on the steep mountain.

George zigged this way and that way, then another way altogether.

He flew over a hill

and landed on the raceway!
"It's a monkey!" yelled a boy, and the crowd cheered.

"Look out, little monkey!" someone yelled from the crowd.

But George was going so fast that the wind roared in his ears, and he could not hear!

But George could see.
He saw a skier right in front of him.
Could he stop?

No!
The crowd gasped as George crashed into the skier and flew up in the air. The skier went tumbling and his ski snapped right in half. When George came down . . .

he landed on the broken ski . . . and kept going!

The crowd was amazed. "What is he doing?" they asked. "Is he skiing? Is he sledding?"

"He's surfing in the snow!" said a boy.

George sailed down the mountain and came to a smooth stop.

What a show! The crowd cheered as George took a bow. No one had seen skiing like this before! When the skier arrived, everyone was glad to see that he was not hurt, and they cheered for him, too. Soon the man with the yellow hat arrived. He was glad to find George.

George was glad to finally find his friend. The man with the yellow hat made his way through the noisy crowd to apologize to the skier. "I'm sorry George caused so much trouble," he said.

"That's okay," said the skier. "I still have another race — and another pair of skis." Then he said, "That was some skiing, George!"

Later that day, the skier raced again — and won! It was a new record! The crowd went wild. They were still cheering when the skier found George at the finish line. "Thanks to you, George, this big crowd stayed to cheer me on," he said. "I couldn't have won without them — or you."

He lifted George to his shoulders and the crowd cheered once more for their favorite monkey skier, George.

The end.